Alive and Ageless

Alive and Ageless

© 2012 by Maxine Kaye

Manufactured in the United States of America

To my three children and eight grandchildren,
for proving that genius can show up even in youth.

Table of Contents

Acknowledgements

In loving gratitude for Dr. Earl Barnum, for showing me the joy of agelessness; Dr. Jane Claypool, wonderful Wise Woman, for encouraging me to share this idea with others and assisting me in making it a reality; Rev. Dr. Cynthia Cavalcanti, for her supreme editorial skills, great artistry, and constant encouragement; Dr. Tom Costa, who reminded thousands, "Don't let age be your cage"; Dr. Anita Richelieu and Dr. Frank Richelieu, for always believing in me; octogenarian Rev. Marian Whiteman and nonagenarian Rev. Kathleen Childress whose advanced youth inspires us all.

Introduction

Welcome to the Real World of Infinite Possibility. The price of admission is your agreement to check your baggage at the door and walk in naked. Once inside, you will find yesterday's sorrow and tomorrow's concern needless. Free of regret and anxiety, you will be able to stand and stretch into the power of this instant— the moment of new creation, your opportunity for real youth.

When you come to know how vital and youthful you are on the deepest level of your being, you will be celebrating your life rather than cursing or regretting it. As you begin to feel even one-tenth of the vigor that is innately yours, you will cease finding excuses for not doing, not going, not fulfilling, and not living your life.

How would you respond if told that you are ageless? How might you explain your physical limitations, your tired legs and fuzzy mind? If you knew—really knew— that you are more than your body, more than your emotions, and much, much more than your intellect, wouldn't you feel encouraged to begin viewing your life from a higher perspective?

The greatest discovery you can make is realizing you are one with a Supreme Life Force that continuously renews Itself by means of you. It is forever available, right where you are, at all times and in all ways. Once you recognize this Power and begin to use It intentionally, your life will take on new meaning, no matter the number of candles on your cake. Men and women who have expanded their awareness of what is possible discover how to bring those possibilities into reality. Those who become intimate with this Life Force and agree to leave their limiting beliefs behind are ready to begin living with real happiness and true freedom.

As the great New Thought minister and teacher, Ernest Holmes, proclaimed, "Your soul belongs to the universe. Your mind is an outlet through which the Creative Intelligence of the universe seeks fulfillment."

Imagine feeling greater health and vitality in your body; enjoying more conscious, loving relationships; seeing a larger expression of your creative talents; and celebrating increased success in every area of your life. In this book, you will read about real people who are doing just that, and their stories will provide you with needed encouragement to drop your limiting beliefs and change every "I can't" to a "Yes, please!" The Life Force is ready and willing to support you on your new journey. You need only open to Its flow and accept Its serene but powerful activity.

The prayer of St. Francis begins, "Lord, make me an instrument of thy peace." It is through the instrument of your own being—physical, emotional, and mental—that the Life Force has the opportunity to reveal Itself and keep you in peace, joy, and aliveness. Just as you needn't try relentlessly to find sufficient oxygen in the air or work hard to keep your blood flowing or your heart beating, you will not find it necessary to struggle with these new concepts or "make" anything happen.

Something within you already knows what is true, and that you are not alone in your awakening to what is possible. You are eternal. You are ageless. Now, it is time to feel alive!

Chapter
One

Boundless Energy

I rafted rivers and climbed mountains in my fifties, scurried up trees and jumped off a telephone pole in my sixties, and in my seventies, I keep a schedule that has been known to tire a teenager. The more I say yes to life, the more life says yes to me. I don't have a secret; I possess a well of inspiration and energy. By the way, you do, too; it's the same one we all have.

Wouldn't you like to access this source of aliveness? Tapping into it is simpler than you might think. We all desire a steady flow of energy moving through our bodies, available for all the ways we choose to direct it each day. Becoming quiet and opening ourselves to this powerful stream of life can clear out those old ideas of insufficiency and awaken us to joy-filled possibilities. Like the hub of a wheel, there is a still point within that allows for greater activity on the outer rim. We have been asleep for a long time, feeling cut off from this life force, and now it's time to wake up!

Age has nothing to do with your ability to access this energy. Charles Fillmore, co-founder of the Unity movement, was in his mid-nineties when he leapt out of his bed and exclaimed, "I fairly sizzle with zeal and enthusiasm, as I spring forth with a mighty faith to do the things that can only be done by me!" He was an amazing man, but his source of energy was the same as yours or mine. His enthusiasm for life came from his deep connection with infinite energy.

It is important to understand that enthusiasm is more than a merely human emotion. Learning how to use this power is something philosophers and healers have known throughout the ages. Gandhi never wavered in his vitality and intense commitment to nonviolent solutions to human conditions. Even with little sleep, he found daily renewal through his passion to make a difference in the world.

The very word *enthusiasm* is derived from the Greek, *en-theos*, or, "in God," the place of infinite power and boundless energy accessible to all. How you choose to use this vital energy in your life is up to you. As Ernest Holmes reminds us, "The Spirit is happy, whole, free, filled with joy, eternal in its existence, and can provide you with everlasting expansion."

Haven't you met twenty-five-year-olds who seemed listless and bored and ninety-year-olds who were alive and vitally participating in their world? Mae West once quipped, "You're never too old to become younger!"

People become tired when they feel disconnected from Source, when they haven't met their purpose and passion for living, and when they've believed too much in what society tells them about ailments and aging. It is essential that we heed Ralph Waldo Emerson's advice to "unlearn the wisdom of the world." No person, no circumstance, and no limited belief can keep us from the natural flow of energy when we go directly to Source and allow ourselves to be filled with enthusiasm.

Of course, as Kahlil Gibran understood, our lives must be balanced with activity and rest. God is a rest and a motion, and so are we. "God rests in reason; God moves in passion," and so do we. I love to sleep deeply and even enjoy an occasional power nap, feeling revitalized in five to ten minutes. I enjoy quiet conversations as much as exuberant hiking or dancing. As we connect consciously with the supreme Life Force and invite the peaceful flow of universal energy to move through our body, our thoughts, our emotions, and our actions, we remain in greater harmony with the Infinite and move serenely and powerfully throughout each day of our lives.

No matter how busy our schedule may appear, we must understand that it is not we of ourselves, but a power greater than we are, that is standing ready to accomplish it all through us. We can feel amazed and thankful at the end of the day, acknowledging the peaceful and effective completion of far more than we may have anticipated.

In my first ministry in Alamo, California, I recall adopting the mantra, "Everything that I do helps me to do everything that I do," especially when facing a crisis-filled day. It reminded me to welcome each activity, realizing it was a steppingstone on my path of accomplishment that day, providing me with more energy and clearer direction toward the next task.

Even a "typical" day included people to counsel, classes to prepare and teach, talks to create, magazine articles to write, telephone calls to return, radio programs to record, meetings with board members and community leaders, and overall administrative duties. I learned to expect the unexpected, like the time I booked two weddings on the same day—one on the Northern California coast and the other in San Francisco's East Bay. Returning from the first wedding, I found myself stuck behind a slow-moving pumpkin truck, deep-breathing and praying I would arrive in time for my next couple. Since I didn't yet have a cell phone, I had to trust that the bride and groom remembered the distance I was driving and were peacefully preparing for their ceremony. They were very pleased when I arrived, and we actually began on time. Had I become frantic behind those pumpkins, I'm sure I would not have brought peace to that wedding—or to myself.

How we react or respond to the unintended, unexpected, unwanted situation has everything to do with the outcome. We can react with fear or anger, raising our blood pressure and being rude to people, or we can respond with a greater intention to move as peacefully as possible through the challenge. What a difference it makes to choose to welcome, rather than resist, whatever we have in front of us to do. Resistance drains energy, whereas acceptance opens the heart to a greater flow of vitality.

Things will happen, e.g., flat tires, pumpkin trucks, a person suddenly in need of our time, and our job is to flow with the changes rather than cursing them. Each day, you really can choose to live that day well, welcoming what is yours to do and knowing you have the energy, calm, and confidence to handle it.

As you rise from your bed or from your meditation chair each morning, consider approaching your day in the following manner:

1. *Gently observe your positive responses or resistive reactions to events that occur during your day.*

2. *Give thanks for your reconnection with a Power greater than you, and allow that Infinite Energy to move you gently through your day.*

3.   *Invite the wisdom within you to select those tasks you intuitively know are right for you by quietly asking, "Is this mine to do?"*

4.   *Decide to live your day enthusiastically, bringing a sense of interest and aliveness to every activity you have chosen.*

5.   *Let the Infinite Energy flow through you harmoniously as you maintain a balance of resting in reason and moving in passion.*

As you consciously choose to live from your center of aliveness, you will find your inner life begins to reflect beautifully in your outer experience—not only as boundless energy, but also as mental and emotional wellbeing and health and beauty in your physical body.

Chapter
Two

Forever Young

Every class I teach, every seminar I lead, and every word I write tends to come out of my own experience of living a life of energy, serenity, creativity, and joy. I find the world interesting, people fascinating, and my life enjoyable and productive. Although I've had my share of challenges, I have not had to overcome major obstacles. I do not attribute this to "good luck" or "great genes," but to a healthy attitude of mind, a balanced emotional life, and a loving acceptance of my physical body.

An ancient writing states the kingdom of Spirit is embodied in the flesh. I agree; hence, my spiritual approach to health and wellbeing includes a belief that there is a Universal Creative Intelligence that activates every cell of my body and keeps me fresh, new, and alive at every age.

The current worldview would have us believe that after a certain birthday, a diminishment of energy and attractiveness sets in and cannot be reversed. My view is that the number of years we have lived has little or nothing to do with our ability to look good, feel good, and live an enjoyable, productive life. The spiritual and practical practices I share with you will contribute greatly to your sense of health, wellbeing, and delight in being alive at any age.

I have no objection to maturing; in fact, I happily celebrate each birthday, feeling wiser and more grateful each year. Every decade has brought fresh awareness, new opportunities, and increased appreciation for what has been, what is to be, and, especially, for the precious moment I am experiencing now. I have found the more present I am, the more peaceful and powerful I feel. Too many people live in the past, reviewing, revisiting, regretting, and regurgitating "the old days," and remaining stuck in ancient history. Others project their thinking into the future, fretting, fearing, fantasizing, and freaking out over unknown but frightening possibilities of what may happen to them. Certainly, an occasional look back in the rear view mirror of life is a helpful way to stay on course, and it is essential to have goals and plans for the future. Still, it is only in this present moment that we are able to make sense of the past and create a happy future.

It is always an honor for me to participate in "life review" with people sharing their stories and recollections of having lived many years on earth. It is even a greater honor to assist them in realizing that each thread of experience has been woven into the tapestry of their lives. As we begin to discover a deeper meaning in each experience and perceive the developing symmetry of events, an essential sense of rightness often lifts us from blame or regret. In making peace with the past, we truly come to value its contributions to our present lives. It is from this place that we make new decisions for today and for the tomorrows to come.

In my own case, I came to realize that the influence my alcoholic father had on the first ten years of my life paled by comparison to the priceless lesson I learned about transformation as I saw him achieve sobriety and remain sober for the rest of his life. The amazement of watching him work his program and help other men with their sobriety far outweighed the sadness and embarrassment of my earlier years. I cherish this firsthand lesson about what can become possible to an awakening human being, and I believe it influenced my decision to enter into the work I do. I often say, "I'm a sucker for transformation!"

Moving out of yesterday's guilt and shame brings great freedom, which, used wisely, invites better choices in this powerful moment. Accepting ourselves as we are, while willingly moving into greater possibilities for every part of our life experience, we finally experience freedom and joy.

You can celebrate your body in this moment, just as it is, and still make improvements in health and appearance. You can appreciate your mind right now, just as it is, and find ways to sharpen your intellect and make smart choices. You can give thanks for your emotions in this very instant, just as they are, and discover how to harmonize and stabilize your emotional life and live in greater balance, peace, and joy.

I love feeling comfortable in my own skin as I go about living this wonderful life in awe and authenticity. An open heart and curious mind contribute to a youthful way of being in this world. Robert Louis Stevenson, in *A Child's Garden of Verses*, writes, "The world is so full of a number of things, I'm sure we should all be as happy as kings." Looking through the eyes of a child, we experience the joy and magic of our surroundings. Imagine awakening each day, ready for discovery and adventure, and feeling fully alive and happy. Children know how to do this because it is completely natural to them. We can relearn the art of curious, joyful living by spending some time each day with young people.

I am intrigued and delighted by my grandchildren's willing and curious approach to each day, and they help me remember to view the world through the fresh eyes of delightful possibilities. A stick becomes a magic wand, mud turns into a cake, and flower gardens provide hours of discovery and wonder. This is our natural state of being, and one to which we can return by choice. It truly is as simple as being willing to open our eyes, our hearts, and our minds and rediscover the childlike delight with which we were born.

Choosing to be alive and aware in the moment is a spiritual practice anyone can embrace at any time of life and in any situation. Even people in unpleasant surroundings or circumstances can find something of beauty, something of value, or something to lift their hearts above their unhappiness or sorrow. A friend once suggested that discipline is loving ourselves enough to do what is good for us, and I appreciate this gentle, clear reminder.

My beloved teacher, Dr. Earl D. Barnum, affectionately known as Barney, taught me very simple yet powerful life lessons. Barney's effective technique for increasing awareness and gently making changes in my thinking or behavior involved the creation of an "observer." There is a significant distinction between noticing and criticizing, and this observer would only act as a "reporter," never a critic. I would ask this imaginary character to inform me politely about a particular thought or action of which I wished to become more aware. I still find it a helpful tool for becoming more aware of my thoughts and actions and making positive changes. Taking responsibility for our healthy life choices is not only essential for our wellbeing, it is our road to true freedom.

We all have the ability to discipline our thinking and to reframe our memories in order to free ourselves to new ways of being. When I was a young child, I spent a great deal of time alone, playing in the gravel-filled back yard of our apartment complex, and I learned to find beauty everywhere. I recall being thrilled by a lone dandelion growing up through the gravel and boasting one rainbow dewdrop; I loved the sparkling colors in that tiny liquid orb. Years later, I realized that although I would occasionally speak of the poor circumstances of my family and the lack of a proper yard and garden, I was still able to find something to lift my heart.

Ironically, when I landscaped my present home in the desert, it included grass, plants, flowers, and several tons of "Desert Gold"—better known as granite. I spent $3,000 and wound up with gravel in my backyard! It seemed very funny to me when I realized this, and everyone knows a healthy sense of humor keeps us young.

Over the years, my spiritual practices have expanded to include many different activities, which I will share with you in the remaining chapters. In truth, I have learned that every precious moment holds the opportunity to experience a sense of the sacred, and keeping the mind focused on the good, the positive, and the life-affirming lifts the heart and clears the mind.

Now in my seventies, I feel every bit as young as I did as a teenager. My interests and activities have changed, but my love of life only increases. Whether I am meditating, doing T'ai Chi or Yoga, exercising, listening to a lecture, having an interesting conversation, playing music, traveling, or enjoying a healthy meal, I feel alive, vital, and youthful.

My beloved Barney's widow, Jenilee Barnum, responds to questions about the number of years she has been on the planet with this wonderful statement: "I am eighteen and a half billion years old and as young as tomorrow." When you realize you are forever young as well, you may wonder why it took you so long to return to your natural state of being.

Why not ask yourself:

1. *Do I find the world an interesting place?*

2. *Do I enjoy my own company and feel comfortable in my own skin?*

3. *Am I able to see beauty in the ordinary and possibilities within difficulties?*

4. *Am I willing gently to notice what I would like to change about myself—without being critical?*

5. *How alive am I feeling right now?*

Chapter Three

Living in the Flow

$\mathcal{O}$ver 2,000 years ago, Lao Tzu stated: "Everything is healthy that flows with the universe..." The continuous flow of a river assures the health of its living inhabitants, and it is only when the water is dammed or polluted that life forms are endangered. You and I are part of a larger system that requires a healthy flow of life's energy, and any attempt to stop its natural movement results in diminished health and wellbeing. Similarly, continual negative input—emotional or mental—tends to affect the purity and effectiveness of this energy in our bodies.

The medical world today is very aware of how our thoughts and feelings impact our bodies. Moreover, a deep sense of connection with something greater than we are tends to bring a healthy sense of peace and wellbeing. Just as a river depends upon its source, we function much more effectively when we connect with the Source of life and its health-giving essence.

My meditation practice has kept me connected to a Peace and a Power greater than I am and allows me to live in the flow of health, inspiration, and vitality. Although we are told, "you can't stop the river," it seems those who try wind up less than healthy and happy. It makes much more sense to identify with this Life Force, inviting and allowing it to lift and inspire us to serene and dynamic living. I have taught meditation classes for over 30 years, and I have witnessed remarkable changes in the lives of people who embrace this practice.

For centuries, teachers of both Western and Eastern traditional meditation practices have assisted students in releasing tension and stress; concentrating more effectively; fine-tuning their bodies, emotions, and minds; increasing awareness; and deepening their connection to a peaceful, powerful Universal Presence. I have seen people reduce the stress in their lives, learn to remain peaceful in challenging situations, increase their receptivity to creative ideas, maintain clarity of mind, sustain emotional balance, and attain a greater sense of physical and spiritual wellbeing through the regular practice of meditation.

You needn't spend hours in meditation to accomplish your goals. Fifteen to 30 minutes in the morning and, ideally, again in the evening, will take you into the serene, dynamic flow of life we all desire for optimum results. Like the refreshment of a good night's sleep on a regular basis, a consistent meditative practice can bring you into a more balanced life of peace and vitality. Allowing yourself to return often to the Source of your life, inviting Its gentle movement in you, being willing to release negative attitudes, and keeping your attention focused on life-affirming thoughts and positive emotions keeps you in the healthy flow of living. As the great teacher of meditation, Roy Eugene Davis, stated, "As a candle flame in a windless spot does not waver, of such is the likeness of a meditator's mind."

I further expanded my appreciation of meditation when I attended the University of California, Berkeley. I was privileged to take a class on mysticism in the Comparative Literature Department from a professor who was intimately associated with Sri Ecknath Easwaren. Easwaren had come to Berkeley as a Fulbright scholar in the 1960s. He fell in love with the students and decided to stay and teach them to meditate, creating the Blue Mountain Meditation Center in Tomales, California.

After months of weekly treks to hear him speak and to meditate with that wonderful group, I realized how helpful the practice could be to my friends on campus. As such, my professor and I decided to establish a "Meditation Club" on campus. Each day at noon, we would gather in a room far above the bustle of campus activity and sit in silent meditation together. Those of us who participated gained much-needed peace and clarity of mind to continue our studies.

I feel quite prepared to move into my morning meditation practice following my T'ai Chi and yoga practices. I like to light a three-tiered candleholder to symbolize the three aspects of my "persona": intellectual, emotional and physical. (I find it significant that actors in ancient Greece spoke their lines through a mask called a "persona." This is the root of our word, "personality," and I see personality as the instrument through which our real nature expresses.)

The lighted candles remind me of the importance of this three-part instrument for the reception and transmission of light. A simple chant can focus and clarify my mind, then I may read or silently recite sacred passages, deepening my sense of connection with Source. Ultimately, I listen from the core of my heart to the Infinite Inspiration waiting to be heard and understood. I often feel so completely loved that tears well.

At times, an answer to a question or challenge may be revealed to me. Offering the instrument of my "persona" to the flow of Higher Wisdom, I simply sit quietly, trusting that the time I take and the intention I bring will reward me later in the day with increased peace, diminished concern, and a few wonderful "ah-ha" moments. I follow this time of deep communion with affirmative prayer for myself and for those who have made requests.

Find the meditation practice that works for you, and be as consistent with it as you can. There are many approaches to meditation, and teachers and groups are available in most areas. If you do not currently have such a practice, here are some simple ideas to help you begin:

1. *Set aside at least 15 minutes in the morning to sit quietly with your back erect and feet on the floor.*

2. *Choose a special place (chair or bench) for this daily activity.*

3. *Close your eyes and focus on your breath, allowing it to become deeper and slower.*

4. *Select a word or short phrase that has meaning for you, such as: Serenity, I Am, or Peace, Be Still. Silently speak and release this seed thought, then continue to focus on your breathing.*

5. *Let every inhalation bring a greater sense of peace and aliveness and allow each exhalation to release any tension or concern.*

6. *Just notice your thoughts, and watch them move on.*

7. *Experience your feelings, and let them go.*

8. Come back often to your breathing, allowing it to bring you into an awareness of the flow of life in and through you.

9. Allow yourself to feel gratitude for giving yourself the gift of this special time as you prepare to enter into your daily activities.

10. Return to the practice in the evening, if possible.

My very wise teacher, Barney, instructed me to "live deeply, not quickly." This has made a great difference in my ability to touch the center of stillness and power within me and to walk it out into my daily experiences.

This conscious intention to become more aligned with the natural rhythm of life tends to slow down the mind, still the body, and harmonize the emotions. Such daily practice provides an opening for the peaceful flow of life, a natural restorer of harmony, energy, and wellbeing. Maintaining equilibrium assists in the ability to respond openly and positively to the experiences of the day, rather than reacting and thereby shutting down the flow of energy. As I learned from Lao Tzu, "Everything is healthy that flows with the universe," and it is a joy to live in this healthy flow of life.

You may wish to ask yourself:

   1.   *Do I desire a deeper connection with the Source of my life?*

   2.   *Am I willing to invest 15 to 30 minutes of my day to feel more love, more peace, and more energy?*

If the answers are "yes," perhaps you would benefit by using the following affirmations to get you started. An "affirmation" is simply a positive statement we make to ourselves to clear out any negative thoughts or beliefs in our subconscious mind. By consciously repeating such statements, we begin the process of releasing what may have been a mental block or an emotional conflict and replacing it with what we truly desire to experience. Why not say to yourself:

   1.   *I dip deeply into the Fountain of Life, open to a peaceful, loving flow of joyful energy moving through me now.*

   2.   *I affirm my intention to let myself be loved deeply, guided serenely, and energized continuously.*

Chapter
Four

Looking Good

A thing of beauty is a joy forever
Its loveliness increases; it will never
Pass into nothingness; but still will keep
A bower quiet for us, and a sleep
Full of sweet dreams, and health, and quiet breathing.

I love the poem, but John Keats did not tell the whole story. Beauty is far more than skin deep; it is the outer expression of something much, much more profound, something within the soul.

Health on the inside cannot help but show up as outer loveliness. In contrast, unresolved anger, tightly-held resentments, and oppressive fear thoughts often result in diminishment of the otherwise healthy glow of aliveness within our bodies. It is from a quiet place of oneness with our Life Source that we allow the healing, transforming energies to flow into the physical.

I recall a funny story about a woman who had extensive plastic surgery—facelift, tummy tuck, breast augmentation, and liposuction—only to return home to find her husband had left her for an older woman! This is definitely a joke with a point, as we tend to go about things backwards by focusing too much on the outer and neglecting the important inner work. Sure, you can have a facelift, but you may benefit even more by a *faith lift!* The great designer, Coco Chanel, said, "Nature gives you the face you have at twenty; it is up to you to merit the face you have at fifty."

While traveling by train in India, Eric Butterworth, a well-known minister and author, was seated across from a striking woman. When he told her how beautiful she was, her eye-opening reply to him was, "Well, I ought to be; I'm nearly 75 years old!" Our culture could learn something about respect for and delight in real maturity and the gifts it can bring.

Although I did not know at the time why I agreed to do it, in my 68th year, I participated in a local, preliminary "Ms. Senior America" pageant in Palm Desert. Rather than a "beauty contest," it was considered "The Age of Elegance," honoring women age 60 years or better. Still, I hesitated participating in something that seemed so foreign to me, and it took several persistent friends a good, long time before I finally acquiesced.

Participants were judged on personal interviews, philosophies of life, formal attire, and talent. While I placed third in the local pageant, the greater "trophy"

I took home was the memory of a woman in her forties who came to me in tears afterward and said, "Now I realize my life has just begun, and I'm finally looking forward to the rest of it!" That's when I knew why I had agreed to enter. Advancing to the state finals, I found the same cooperative spirit and joy of being alive in those women.

There was, however, one instance of collective envy for a particular contestant—a woman in her eighties with the legs of a 20-year-old! She was also talented enough to have designed and sown her own outfit, and she did place in the top three that day. Oh, for those legs!

The grace of mature women seems to include genuine appreciation for one another and a real desire that each do well. We helped each other dress, applauded enthusiastically for each one's performance, and complimented one another at every opportunity. Any bit of nervousness was met with cheerful assurance and loving support from the others. There was not only a great pool of talent, but a wealth of gracious living and outstanding community contributions in that group of amazing women, plus a relaxed attitude of mutual caring, appreciation, and humor.

Our group included classically-trained singers, dancers, and even a former television personality. The audience experienced an awakening to the joy of aliveness and the ability to be creative, beautiful, elegant, and inspiring at any age. We experienced a deeper appreciation for ourselves and for this wonderful time of life in which we are free to live beautifully and love it!

Participating in the state pageant, I took my place proudly among mature and capable women. We knew how to look good, feel good, and act from goodness by making positive contributions to the world. We also knew how to focus on our inner qualities, like so many great teachers and philosophers. Socrates was not known to be physically attractive; yet in Plato's dialogue, "Phaedrus," we read his prayer to the gods: "Dear Pan, and all ye other gods that dwell in this place, grant that I may become fair within, and that such outward things as I have may not war against the spirit within me."

In the words of Confucius, "Everything has its beauty, but not everyone sees it." It is time we began to bring forth the beauty from within ourselves by recognizing how very present it is and then being willing to share it with the world. Consider these possibilities to begin the process:

1. *Realize that beauty, as a universal attribute, is present everywhere.*

2. *Begin to notice beauty and elegance in your world: in nature, art, music, and people.*

3. Make a list of what is beautiful and graceful about yourself, both inside and out, acknowledging and appreciating your uniqueness.

4. Daily, release at least one resentment and replace it with something you appreciate.

5. Smile more, starting with your very own image in the mirror.

There are many effective practices you can follow to enhance and maintain the joy of "looking good," but it truly begins with the rediscovery of your inner light, your radiant being, and your unique and beautiful self. Estée Lauder said, "Beauty is an attitude. There's no secret." Some people choose to bathe in exotic oils each day, while others immerse themselves in the joy of aliveness! Who says you can't do both?

Chapter Five

Conscious Eating

$\mathcal{M}$ost people's food choices change as they become more aware of those selections that add to health and wellbeing and those that may diminish it. Over the years, I have developed a balanced and healthy relationship to food, choosing to fuel my body more with fresh, whole foods and doing my best to avoid highly-processed or refined ones. Each body type is unique and may require different kinds of nourishment to maintain it well, so there is no universal eating plan that is appropriate for everyone.

Although my weight has not fluctuated much over the years (except, of course, for those three pregnancies!), I know that in the past, during challenging or stressful periods, I had a tendency to substitute comfort foods for comforting thoughts and feelings. Now, I realize a stir-fry of organic veggies, tofu, and brown rice is a meal that comforts me emotionally while nourishing me physically. I do not call myself a vegetarian but a *flexitarian*, listening to my body and enjoying whatever I have chosen to eat at the moment. I recently discovered the delight of raw vegan food—filled with healthy enzymes that assist the body in feeling even more energized—and have enjoyed delicious, nutritious food prepared by a wonderful "un-cook!"

Tending toward a vegetarian diet, eating slowly, enjoying smaller meals more frequently during the day, and being willing to stop eating when my "full button" goes on assist me in maintaining a healthy weight and keep my energy flowing. Plus, I like to be conscious of what I am selecting, how I am preparing it, and, most of all, my attitude while I am eating the meal.

Years ago, we were admonished, "You are what you eat." Later, Jack Schwarz wrote a book entitled, *It's Not What You Eat, but What Eats You.* Although I have not read it, I love the concept that our thoughts and feelings have a greater impact on our bodies than the foods we ingest. If I decide to indulge in a type of food I rarely eat, I simply enjoy it without guilt, knowing my regular practices provide a healthy framework within which an occasional digression is not a transgression.

Prayers of gratitude are usually heard around the Thanksgiving table and, in many households, *grace* is spoken daily at family meals. I once heard a wise and rascally older minister proclaim, "It helps with the digestion!" There may well be something to the idea of agreeing with our food so it doesn't disagree with us! Kahlil Gibran believed consuming food could become "an act of worship," suggesting:

And when you crush an apple with your teeth, say to it in your heart,
Your seeds shall live in my body,
And the buds of your tomorrow shall blossom in my heart,
And your fragrance shall be my breath,
And together we shall rejoice through all the seasons.

We can develop the simple practice of regarding our food with respect and appreciation, welcoming the energy and comfort it brings, and enjoying it fully as we receive it consciously and gratefully. Preferring the fullness of heart to the fullness of belly, I find my choices more intelligent and appropriate when I enjoy my meals with gratitude and respect.

As you become more aware of your body type, lifestyle, and preferences, you can easily develop an approach to eating that works well to keep you feeling alive and vital. The key is to become more conscious as you change your relationship to food. You might like to see how you respond to the following questions and statements:

1. *Which foods tend to make me feel lighter?*

2. *Which foods tend to make me feel energized?*

3. *Food is my friend.*

4. *I like the way my body looks.*

5. *I am ready to feel more conscious around food.*

6. *I am ready to express gratitude for my meals.*

As you listen to your responses openly and honestly, you will have a clearer idea about what to change or embrace regarding your relationship with food. Developing a personal program for greater freedom and vitality begins with creating and accepting a new image of yourself and allowing it to bring you a greater sense of confidence in your new, healthier choices. Remember, "Discipline is loving yourself enough to do what is good for you."

Below are some positive ideas to you with the changes you wish to make. Why not say to yourself:

1. *I listen to the Wisdom in me that guides my healthy, conscious choices.*

2. *I am grateful for the food I eat, agreeing to agree with its goodness.*

3. *I taste and enjoy my food, eating only as much as I need.*

4. *I allow the nutrients to energize and vitalize my body.*

5. *I give thanks for my wise choices and delight in the freedom they bring.*

Chapter
Six

The Joy of Movement

The flow of Infinite Energy through our bodies is natural and essential to our health and vitality. Movement increases both physical flexibility and emotional and mental wellbeing. Some people enjoy working out at a gym, while others swim, cycle, walk, hike, dance, employ martial arts, or find other interesting ways to move and keep the dynamic flow of life circulating.

My longtime morning practice includes T'ai Chi and Yoga, and the versions of each, learned years ago, fit nicely with my daily schedule as I prepare to enter into meditation. Although I usually enjoy my T'ai Chi movements on the patio and my Yoga stretches in a particular room in my home, both are completely portable and I can do them anywhere I happen to be. This is also true of walking, hiking, and the other exercise I enjoy. Additionally, I prefer stairs to elevators!

I walk at a fast pace at least two miles per day and usually a minimum of five days a week. Though I always enjoy an old-fashioned walk with a friend, exploring a garden or looking in store windows, that is not what my energizing walks are about! If you were to join me in this morning exercise, you might need long legs and good lungs, as I move in joyful energy and keen aliveness with each stride. All the while, I silently repeat a mantra in rhythm with my step, even as I enjoy the scenery and delight in the fragrance of the flowers I pass.

Usually twice a week, I incorporate a combination of sit-ups and stretching exercises designed by two chiropractors. The routine was created to firm the abdominal muscles and keep the entire body strong and flexible while being very kind to the spine. It requires rubber tubes for stretching, and these find their way into my luggage alongside my walking shoes every time I travel.

Hiking is great exercise and can be temperate or vigorous, depending on the area chosen and the individual's abilities. Benefits beyond physical fitness include the discovery of new vistas and the delight of experiencing the serenity of nature, away from city noise and congestion. Didn't we love exploring new regions when we were children?

Imagine entering into the magic again by hiking up a hill with your walking stick and noticing a hawk flying overhead or a family of quail parading on the trail in front of you! Climbing a hill or mountain provides more than physical exercise, as Duke Senior expresses in *As You Like It*, "And this our life, exempt from public haunts, finds tongues in trees, books in running brooks, sermons in stones and good in everything."

The famous naturalist, John Muir, did not care for the word "hiking," preferring to use *saunter*, a French word describing pilgrimages during the Middle Ages. Muir's reason for this choice was said to have come from a time when people in the villages asked the pilgrims where they were going, and they replied, "A la sainte terre," meaning to the holy land. Muir once chided, "Now these mountains are our Holy Land, and we ought to saunter through them reverently, not 'hike' through them." He was so aware of the all-encompassing benefits of aligning our body, mind, and spirit with nature that he stated, "Everybody needs beauty as well as bread, places to play in and pray in, where nature may heal and give strength to body and soul alike."

Whether you move your body to music, lob a tennis ball across the court, trot a horse up a trail, swim laps in a pool, hit a golf ball on the green, or walk, hike, or saunter on a nature path, you know the joy you feel as you experience the rhythm of the universe moving through you and expanding your awareness of aliveness in every cell of your body.

Whatever your current physical activities may be, and however equipped you feel to add to them, you might consider the following in determining what will best serve you. Why not ask yourself:

1. *What kind of activity makes me feel more alive?*

2. *Am I willing to engage in more physical movement each day?*

3. *How much time would I like to devote to these practices?*

4. *What type of exercise might benefit me mentally and spiritually as well?*

5. *Am I willing to align myself more deeply with the flow of life in my body?*

Even a few minutes of planned physical activity each day can bring benefits of increased strength and flexibility while providing a sense of adventure, accomplishment, and overall wellbeing. Why not say to yourself:

1. *I enjoy feeling the flow of life's energy through my body.*

2. *I move to the rhythm of the universe.*

3. *I invite the Wisdom within me to choose the exercise that is right for me.*

4. *I love and appreciate my body and its increasing energy.*

5. *I am grateful for the joyous freedom of movement I now experience.*

Chapter Seven

Impossible Dreams

Although it was Thoreau's opinion that most people ". . . live lives of quiet desperation," I have observed growing evidence to the contrary. I see people awakening to infinite possibilities by realizing their dreams and fulfilling their heart's desires at any age. Later, in the chapter entitled "Encouraging Examples," you will read of people who have achieved amazing accomplishments in their later years. Their firsthand accounts of physical feats, academic achievements, personal growth, and finding love again provide inspiration and motivation.

Deferred dreams can be taken from the shelf, no matter how many years they have been stored there. When we raise them to the light of consciousness, we bring new life to ourselves.

I was in my late forties when I decided to return to school to commence a Field Major in Humanities, focusing on Ancient Greek Civilization. Already an ordained minister, I was sometimes asked, "What are you going to do with that?" It was not about *doing* anything *with* it, but about following a passion and enjoying a deeper understanding of certain cultural roots. From world-class professors, I took courses in Greek philosophy, religion, art, literature, architecture, and archeology. I completed two semesters of the Attic Greek language, graduating from the University of California, Berkeley, just before my fiftieth birthday—magna cum laude! I took myself to Greece for three weeks, *sauntering* through museums, exploring archeological sites, practicing modern Greek with the locals, and seeing and experiencing what I had dreamed about for years. I suppose that's what I "did with" my education!

Many people achieve so-called impossible dreams, despite others' doubts. I read about a woman named Helen Haas in Desert Hot Springs, California, who received her Master's degree in Pastoral Ministry from Boston University on May 19, 2008. She celebrated her graduation and her eightieth birthday at the same time!

Hazel Soares graduated from Mills College in Oakland, California, at age 94, saying, "It's taken me quite a long time because I've had a busy life." She also commented, "There's no reason why you could not go back . . . once you try it, it's exciting to go to school." Hazel, who has six children and more than 40 grandchildren and great grandchildren, earned an art history degree then began working as a docent at a local art museum. She attained a lifelong desire and continued by giving her gift to others.

When I met my neighbors, Anita and John, she was 80 and he was 85. During the time they lived nearby, Anita moved through a cancer experience then published two novels. John discovered his talent as an artist and sculptor, and his work is shown in upscale galleries.

The poet, Ella Wheeler Wilcox, knew about reaching and attaining. She wrote:

> *That which the upreaching spirit can achieve*
> *The grand and all-creative forces know;*
> *They will assist and strengthen as the light*
> *Lifts up the acorn to the oak tree's height.*
> *Thou has but to resolve, and lo! God's whole*
> *Great universe shall fortify thy soul.*

Creativity has no expiration date. Life's urge to move through us in new and interesting ways never ceases, and it is time we relinquished all those erroneous beliefs about limitation or insufficiency, particularly with regard to age. The "upreaching spirit" within us knows only to express; it cannot be constricted by anything except the mental or emotional blocks we place in its path. I have learned to trust the universe, as it has always supported me in realizing *impossible dreams* the moment I moved into *possibility thinking*.

Be ready to find encouragement even from surprising sources. Once you have set the intention to allow a dream to be fulfilled, the universe finds a way to help you.

While attending UC Berkeley, I spent a good amount of time in Dwinelle Hall, since many Classics courses were taught there, including languages like Ancient Greek. My Attic Greek class was, without question, the most difficult of all my coursework. One day, after a particularly confusing lesson, I was leaving the building with a frown on my face and Greek participles dangling from my ears. Descending the steps, I saw a familiar Berkeley character in the quad. He was known as "The Polka-Dot Man," for he always dressed in polka-dot shirt, trousers, and shoes and often carried a polka-dot umbrella. He would walk in measured steps, as if on military drill, carrying a stick or his folded umbrella before him, and never uttering a word. On this day, as I walked down to the quad and seriously doubted my ability to grasp the nuances of an ancient language, William, the Polka-Dot Man, stopped his parade, walked directly to me, looked me in the eye, and exclaimed, "Wake up, Wonder Woman! Wake up!"

When we are open to inspiration, even from unlikely people and situations, we begin to realize there is more support for our dreams and desires than we may have believed. There is a bigger picture, a universal law that responds to our internal choices and decisions. Some have called this the Law of Attraction. Regardless of what we call it, this law brings about what we consistently think about and focus on.

Being open to inspiration includes a willingness to be encouraged by other people's accomplishments without comparing our interests or abilities to theirs. It was a big deal for me to climb Mt. Shasta in my late forties, as I had never before held an ice axe or even heard of *pitons,* much less had them attached to my boots. This adventure with more seasoned mountain climbers brought me a keener awareness of the way I deal with difficulties and an enormous appreciation for team support and the spirit of courage within us all to keep moving one step at a time toward our goals. After a long and particularly challenging ascent through a surprise snowstorm, one of the professional mountaineers on the climb encouraged us to continue by reminding us of Aesop's *The Tortoise and the Hare:* "Slow and steady," he said, "wins the race."

Years later, I read how Dara Torres, at age 41, was heading for her fifth Olympics after winning both the 50- and 100-meter freestyles in the 2008 trials. She had given birth just two years previously and had undergone two surgeries within the previous eight months. Every opportunity to let life be magnificent in us is an inspiration to others to allow their dreams to come true, too.

We all need a supportive team of people who are willing and able to supply the inspiration needed for us to go on, even when things are looking down. I am deeply grateful to all my mentors, and many are available to you, as well. Just look around for people who are achieving dreams like yours. Even if you never meet them, you can let their success motivate you to continue. The people in your life who see how committed you are to your heart's desire are likely to add more support to your vision than you may think.

Years ago, I was the guest speaker for a congregation in Vallejo, California. My message that morning included the idea that we need to live from our greater potential so as not to ignore the music within, figuratively speaking. Invited back the following year, I was met by an enthusiastic woman who told me she had taken my words literally and formed a musical band that was now flourishing!

Why not find out what is possible for you? I was drawn to the idea of trying a ropes course as a way to develop teamwork and increase self-confidence. At 66, I joined a few of my colleagues at a mountain retreat. Working in concert with one another, we climbed tall trees and walked in tandem across high wires. The highlight for me was the leap off the telephone pole I had climbed, successfully catching and swinging on a trapeze before my friends lowered me to the ground.

This success took place after I slipped and fell part way down the pole on the first try. As I scrambled back to the top, the leader shouted up, "Maxine, did you want to go again?" I replied, "Yes, please!" fired with new enthusiasm to make it this time, and I did. This phrase became a motto for my congregation, especially when we wanted to move forward with a new plan or idea. "Yes, please!" is a dynamic way to live our lives, as it opens up possibilities we may otherwise miss. Maybe jumping off telephone poles is not on your to-do list, but I'm sure plenty of other dreams are!

Some metaphysicians in the early twentieth century were fond of saying, "Nothing is too good to be true; nothing is too wonderful to happen to you." How can we know which direction to take our innate creativity? Is there a litmus test to determine if something we desire is right for us? The Creative Intelligence within us must express, and It has multitudinous ways in which to do so. Ernest Holmes posed this simple yet profound question: "Does the thing I wish to do express more life, more happiness, more peace to myself, and at the same time harm no one? If it does, it is right."

Why not ask yourself the following:

1. *What did I love to do as a child that delighted my heart and gave me a sense of joy?*

2. *Are there dreams I have deferred that I now want to take down from the shelf and reexamine?*

3. *If I had all the necessary resources and required permission from no one, what would I choose to do today?*

4. *Am I willing to move from the frustration of an "impossible dream" to the satisfaction of an accomplished goal?*

5. *What do I choose?*

Connecting with a power greater than you, yet right where you are, you can begin by allowing it to guide you into greater fulfillment by focusing your attention on real possibilities. Why not say to yourself:

1. *The Creative Intelligent Activity of the Universe is at work within me.*

2. *I am a Center for this Creative Expression.*

3. *I develop and use my true talents and abilities.*

4. *I am supported by a great Power in all I do.*

5. *I am right on time, all the time, allowing joyous activity to express through me.*

Chapter
Eight

Transforming Outworn Beliefs

$\mathcal{M}$any years of visits to skilled nursing and assisted living facilities have provided me with rich insights into how beliefs and behaviors not only develop early in life but become more pronounced as time goes by. I began to question whether those clients who resisted change, had unrealistic expectations, or tended to complain loudly and unnecessarily had recently begun those behaviors or whether they had been part of their conduct for some time. Similarly, I wondered whether those who adapted easily to new people and surroundings and brought a spirit of cooperation to each day had long been accustomed to living that way.

Years later, to my delight, I heard an explanation taken from the book, *The More-So Principle,* that was right in line with my conclusion that what we believe, and, therefore, how we behave, tends to perpetuate itself as we mature unless and until we choose to make changes. It basically stated that happy people were probably happy in their earlier years and became even happier over time. Disgruntled people likely thought life was bleak when they were younger and became even more disgruntled through the years. I see this as a "cautionary tale," awakening us to the necessity of observing negative beliefs, attitudes, and actions in order to choose differently; otherwise, we are likely to become "more-so."

Deepak Chopra wrote, "The development of any character trait starts early in life and begins to display itself by middle age. The best way to ensure that you will be adaptable in old age is to work on being that way while you are still young." Gandhi explained the phenomenon in this way: "Your beliefs become your thoughts, your thoughts become your words, your words become your actions, your actions become your habits, your habits become your values, and your values become your destiny."

To move into an expanded sense of ourselves and live in freedom and joy at any age, we must be willing to release that which no longer serves us, and this activity begins in the mind. The moment we identify the beliefs that limited us and kept us small, we have the opportunity to see the negative thinking that brought them into being.

At that point of understanding, we can choose to let them go and replace them with life-giving, productive, affirming ideas. Affirm means to *make firm*, and what a joy it is to release unworkable beliefs and accept and solidify the healthy ideas of possibility within ourselves.

Society is becoming more receptive to *aliveness at any age,* primarily because maturing men and women are providing us with so much living evidence of physical strength and flexibility, mental clarity and acuity, and emotional balance and satisfaction. We who love life and are living it fully are no longer the exception, but the rule. If you are ready to step up to new possibilities, you may consider taking a gentle look inside your belief system to see which outworn or unworkable beliefs you are ready to discard. Then, you can decide what fits nicely with your new lifestyle. Letting go of fear and embracing joy is a powerful beginning to your new mode of aliveness and agelessness.

Although you may wish to work with a partner, spiritual counselor, or trusted friend on the following exercises, a sincere desire to move out of limitation and into freedom can provide the needed impetus to begin making these changes on your own. Even then, you may become aware that a Power greater than you is wisely and lovingly supporting and guiding you on this journey. This Presence, which has always been with you, encourages you to reclaim your life. Ernest Holmes wisely stated, "One, alone, in consciousness with the Infinite, constitutes a complete majority.

Knowing this in your thought, work in perfect peace and calm. Always expect the good!"

The suggested format for this exercise is to identify an error belief and release it, then replace it with an affirmative statement of truth. Below are a couple of ideas to get you started. Begin with a clean sheet of paper, and let the thoughts and feelings flow without editing them. Ultimately, your list of error beliefs will be discarded and the affirmations placed where you can read and embody them daily. For example:

1a. *Old Belief:* I used to believe I would lose physical strength and mental agility as I got older.

1b. *New Belief:* I now affirm that Life is infinitely powerful, flexible, and alive as It flows through me, renewing me in grace, vitality, and vigor.

2a. *Old Belief:* I used to believe I would become less interesting to others as I aged.

2b. *New Belief:* I now affirm that my mind is part of the Infinite Mind, that I think and speak with fresh ideas and insights, and that I am valuable and interesting to others.

After completing this exercise, discard the list of outworn beliefs and place the affirmations in a place you will see them often, speaking the new ideas aloud each day. When you discover other limiting beliefs still operating within you, do this exercise again, writing and speaking the new affirmations daily.

This simple activity is more effective than you realize, and the best part is that you become aware of the power of your personal choices! You and I are larger than any belief system. Choosing anew and watching the changes take place confirms that you are more powerful than the old thought patterns and that Life Itself supports and celebrates you as you choose new thought patterns and return to your natural state of aliveness and joy.

I heard of a woman who begins each day with Walt Whitman's words:

> *Afoot and lighthearted I take to the open road,*
> *Healthy, free, the world before me,*
> *The long brown path before me,*
> *leading wherever I choose.*

Chapter
Nine

Creative Connections

The sooner we are able to establish our deep connection to all Life and to one another, the more fulfilling our individual life experience will become. There is a vast difference between loneliness and aloneness. It is possible to be with a group and still feel lonely when you lack personal connections or a positive sense of self. On the other hand, it is possible to be solely in your own company and feel no loneliness at all.

Having healthy relationships with others begins with having a healthy sense of self; it includes savoring those sweet moments of aloneness, finding ways to reconnect and recharge. Honoring each person's individual make-up and determining the quality of connectedness present in our lives, we can establish a balance between enjoying our own company and appreciating relationships with others.

Although most of us were not designed to be hermits, I do enjoy a good deal of quiet time, connecting to my Source through meditation and creative activities that do not involve other people. These opportunities provide me with such energy and aliveness that I am happy to involve myself with others for long periods of time. I adore visits with my children and grandchildren, creative activities with dear friends, working in a class or seminar with people I appreciate getting to know on a deeper level, or visiting a new area and delighting in meeting perfect strangers. Only you know the optimum balance of quiet introspection and outer connection for yourself.

I have noticed that some people begin to retreat from life when they have experienced many losses, including estrangement from family members, and I have seen these people begin to wither rather than find a way to reconnect and discover value in their lives. I have also seen many people deal effectively with their sorrows, court a comforting Presence within themselves, and begin to bring more life to their lives.

I recall a very lonely woman who began volunteering in a local hospital's newborn nursery, feeding and rocking babies and filling up her own "love sponge" as well as theirs. As humans, we seem to experience something called "skin hunger," and it is only natural that we desire to hold and be held. This condition tends to result from a person going too long without human touch, as touching and being touched is a basic human need. It is the adult version of the failure to thrive (FTT) syndrome experienced by some babies who are not cuddled and held enough, and it often occurs after the loss of a loved one or during a protracted communicable illness. There just may be something to the daily minimum requirement of hugs and even occasional or regular massage.

The possibilities of significant involvement in life are endless. Whether rescuing animals, teaching a child to read, becoming a docent at a museum, organizing a block party, taking a class at a community college, or finding a special partner to love. As Robert Fulghum advised, we can and must discover ways to "hold hands and stick together." Isolation is always a choice, though not always a wise one.

It appears we entered into this world on our own personal journey and shall depart from it on our own as well; yet, there are helpers and companions along the way. As adults, we ultimately come to appreciate the value of participating with others, both as givers and receivers.

I have been privileged to maintain a friendship with several women from my childhood, a few actually going all the way back to grammar school. We were Girl Scouts together, then became Mariner Scouts, learning to sail and taking memorable trips to Catalina Island from Redondo Beach, California. Since we were sponsored by a yacht club, we had the joy of "crewing" on beautiful sailboats. After all these years, we continue our special connection, even though we no longer live in the same area, and we gather in various locations each year or so. Six of the original seven remain, and even our Mariner Scout leader joins us whenever she can. As different as our lives have become, we share a very precious bond and find our mutual respect and appreciation grows greater with each year.

Whether our companions are human or animal, there is great delight and comfort in forming such connections. Some time ago, I adopted a precious little dog. Although I had no conscious desire to bring an animal into my life, I quickly discovered our mutual delight in being in one another's company. It is a serious responsibility, and it takes more thought and planning now that a "fur person" lives with me, but it is an enriching experience, and my pup, Yoga, makes every day an adventure. I named her when she began stretching and rolling over during my morning Yoga routine the first day she was with me. I have learned much about relationships from her, and these lessons can easily be translated into human connections. We really listen to one another and enjoy mutual respect, and affection. Not everyone needs a dog or cat, but I apparently did.

You may wish to use the following questions to assess your needs for inner and outer connection, then consider making some different choices about your lifestyle. Why not ask yourself:

1. *How much do I enjoy my own company, and am I comfortable in my own skin?*

2. *Am I spending sufficient time in quiet meditation, feeling connected to my Source, and have I found a group of like-minded people with whom I may share this experience?*

3. *How am I dealing with loss, such as death of a loved one or estrangement from a friend or family member?*

4. *Am I willing to move through grief, feeling my authentic feelings and allowing myself to discover ways to use the pain to help others?*

5. *Have I found a bereavement group to assist me through the process?*

6. *Do I extend myself to my loved ones, suggesting interesting activities we may share yet not retreating into myself if they are not available?*

7. *Am I willing to volunteer in areas that interest me, knowing I can make a difference in my world?*

8. *When I need to be held, do I allow myself to feel a Divine Embrace, do I find a willing hugger to hug, or possibly snuggle a child or pet?*

9. *Do I engage in new and fascinating activities that delight me and make me an even more interesting person?*

10. *Am I extending my circle of caring allies, and am I learning to be a wonderful friend?*

It really does begin within our own hearts and minds, and you might be amazed to find you are capable of releasing even ancient animosities and freeing yourself to the joy of living with other beloved beings in this world. As you find the optimum balance between your inner connection and your outer connections, you might consider Edwin Markham's remarkable poem, "Outwitted":

> *He drew a circle that shut me out—*
> *Heretic, rebel, a thing to flout.*
> *But Love and I had the wit to win:*
> *We drew a circle that took him in.*

Opening your heart to the creative activity of forgiving, loving, and celebrating others is very likely to assist in creating a harmonious balance of inner and outer life. You and I are inextricably connected to Life and to each other and can develop healthier relationships.

Chapter Ten

Love, Value, and Creativity

Of the many "supposed" psychological needs we have as human beings, Karen Horney, M.D., has suggested there exist three "real" ones: (1) To love and to be loved; (2) to feel worthwhile to yourself and at least one other person; and, (3) to be creative.

I agree with all three and believe each one contributes to a healthy expression of living at any age. Let's begin with the first need.

Loving and being loved seem as important as the physiological need for air. Note that in both cases, there is reciprocity, as the cycle of breathing and the cycle of loving necessitate requital. Try breathing in then holding your breath and refusing to release it; or, exhale then attempt not to inhale again. It is not possible, for breathing is a natural, reciprocal flow, and we are not able to stop it until the day we die. Interestingly, we do not need to inhale and exhale exactly the same air to maintain this perfect balance.

Similarly, love must flow through us if we are to be healthy and content, and expressing love and receiving love do not necessarily have to involve the same person. Love flows most easily when shared without specific expectations of an immediate return from the recipients toward whom we direct it. Objectiveless love is the purest, easiest, and most effective energy, as no object is required to invite and allow its flow.

I truly know that I must love, that it is natural for me to express it, and that I am not happy if I attempt to withhold it. I also am aware that the experience of feeling loved, so necessary to all sentient beings, is essential to my happiness.

Imagine making a conscious decision to let love flow from your heart every day and to be willing to receive love back into your heart. Believe it or not, it really can be that simple.

Start with the people already in your life. Quietly become aware of all their wonderful qualities, then silently send waves of love to each one. Think about the gifts they have brought to you, even those that seemed challenging, and just let love move out from your heart without any expectations at all. Next, allow unconditional love to move out to all people and all sentient beings in the world. Beginning this exercise when you are alone, then walking into your day with a sense of being a "recirculating fountain of love" can bring happy surprises to you. This is not because you have changed anyone, but because you have opened your heart to more loving possibilities.

For some people, the next part of this exercise is more difficult, i.e., allowing yourself to be loved. Anyone who has ever felt hurt or disappointed and reacted by isolating or mistrusting may understand the difficulty of letting love in even while desperately desiring it.

Scientific studies have shown how infants who are given food but do not receive loving touch and nurture fail to thrive and can die. We never move beyond this essential need to be loved, comforted, and cared for, even though we may devise clever strategies for pretending not to require such. Some people learn to receive love from significant others, some from family and friends, and some from a Loving Presence that may be called God.

Whether you are single or in an intimate relationship, the flow of love continues to be essential for optimal health. For myself, I maintain a very healthy flow of love, whether or not I am in a close relationship. I loved each of my three (yes, three) husbands and have enjoyed a number of other relationships in my life. Another discovery I have made about agelessness is that whether I have been older, younger, or close in age to men in my life, each relationship was quite special and had absolutely nothing to do with numbers. It has everything to do with aliveness, which we can experience at any time, place, or age.

I adore my three children and eight grandchildren and am grateful for them all. Even if a misunderstanding arises, I have learned to maintain the feeling of love I have for each one, and I know they love me even if they do not say so in the moment. You see, loving and being loved truly are choices, and this great news keeps us from being disappointed by any other person. I prefer the sweet feeling of positive, respectful connection with everyone I may meet and am grateful I do not have to wait for him or her to begin it.

I also enjoy recognizing the gifts I have given to and received from past relationships in my life. I not only wish to grant harmless passage through my mind to each one, I choose to feel gratitude that they have been or continue to be a part of my journey. Again, it is a choice to give and receive love, and doing so keeps us young and healthy. I'll take a sense of appreciation over one of resentment any day.

Let's look at the second real need, which is to feel worthwhile to yourself and at least one other person. It isn't really necessary to become the president of your company or earn fame or notoriety in the world to enjoy a sense of great value. You can feel good about yourself simply by considering how very special you are. We have heard all our lives that each individual is so unique there is no one exactly like anyone else. Even twins have different fingerprints. You really are irreplaceable and might benefit by realizing what this means to you. I have known people who had difficulty understanding this, as no one had ever told them they were wonderful. The most striking example of this comes from my work in prison ministry.

For two years, I visited men's modules of a local jail for a few hours each week and had many eye-opening experiences. Even though many of the men were reluctant to meet with me at first, I eventually had groups of 20 or so who were hungry to have someone see them as significant human beings. It amazed and grieved me to find that some had never heard one positive thing about themselves and had no expectation of enjoying a meaningful life. It amazed and delighted me to find that my consistency in treating them with care and respect began to awaken many of them to different possibilities. As they were able see that they were far more than their behaviors and much greater than what they had learned from their environment, they began to connect with a deeper, truer sense of their value.

This respect became mutual, and I always felt honored and highly regarded when I was with them. Like the circulation of love and caring, the recognition of value flows in both directions. Perhaps you can think of someone in your life who does not feel an innate sense of worth. You may wish to apply the principle by standing in silent witness to his or her inner core, willing to look beyond external behaviors long enough to find common ground. The more you are willing to perceive the true value of others, the easier it becomes to be aware of your own.

Honoring your unique worth also opens you to the third authentic need, i.e., to be creative. I have seen people of all ages discovering and using talents of which they were not aware until they began to see themselves in a new light. Grandma Moses was not the only person of advanced age to stun the world with her art! Our creativity need not express through painting or music or dancing or writing; it is important to get in touch with our own unique ability.

Have you never felt an inner urge for a new idea to be born in you? Whether it is inventing a delicious recipe, building a table or chair, or developing a healthy relationship, you can flow with creativity by saying, "Yes, please," to such an idea. I have seen the willingness to bring forth newness actually add life to people's living, and I know how effective it is for me. It is so entertaining for me to invite friends or family to dinner and serve them delicious, innovative recipes

I have not even pretested. Even more enjoyable is deciding to bring love, compassion, and understanding to a relationship that may have seemed difficult and to see and feel the changes a little creativity can bring.

I have had the extreme pleasure of changing challenging work situations into respectful and pleasant daily exchanges simply by refusing to react to a person's attitude and raising my own instead. Looking past someone's behavior and finding something to appreciate allows me to create an atmosphere of genuine caring. Responding to the heart of a person, rather than reacting to words or behaviors, is a very creative way to establish a healthy workplace.

Love can flow deliciously at any age, especially as we acknowledge our own worth and see the value in others. You were born to love and to be loved, to feel worthwhile to yourself and many other people, and to allow the Creative Intelligence of the universe to fill you with bright ideas that keep you young and vital.

Why not ask yourself:

1. *Am I as loving as I would like to be?*

2. *Am I willing to forgive past hurts and regrets in order to let love flow unconditionally?*

3. *Do I feel as loved as I would like to feel?*

4. Am I willing to become a "generous receiver" of love by opening my heart to conscious relationships?

5. Do I really know my worth, and am I willing to see the value in others?

6. Am I open to new, creative ideas, and am I enthusiastic about bringing them into my life?

Why not say to yourself:

1. I am a recirculating Fountain of Love.

2. I forgive readily and choose compassion and understanding.

3. I replace regret with gratitude.

4. I am a very valuable, worthwhile person.

5. I am creative, intelligent, and joyful, always bringing newness into my life.

Chapter Eleven

Meaning and Purpose

Watch a small child go about the business of his or her day, and you will see what it looks like to enter into each activity with purpose. He will not stop making mud pies until there is one for every member of his family. She paints a picture, adding the family dog to complete the masterpiece. The innate imagination and enthusiasm of each little person can carry over into adulthood and keep us youthful and happy if we maintain the interest and joy that are natural to us all.

Too often, people experience a kind of "identity crisis," confusing what they do with who they are. Confining ourselves to such labels tends to diminish the sense of freedom to delight in any activity we may choose. You may have a title of CEO or be known as a jazz musician or homemaker, but the essence of who you really are, who you always have been, is so much larger than any definition that it cannot be contained in a label. It is the spirit in you that has made choices throughout your life regarding how you express that spirit. There is no limit to how you may show up in the world.

When I realized it was time to leave my congregation in Los Altos, California, I was clear it was not to be a retirement, so the dear people there gave me a fabulous *re-wirement* party. Isn't it wonderful to continue reinventing ourselves at any time in life?

A few months later, I found myself in Palm Desert, California, having answered an inner call to make a major move and an outer call to serve with the new pastor of a thriving congregation. Who knew? Something in me obviously did, and it continued to be a fulfilling experience for six years. Then I realized it was, once again, time to "re-wire!" In all my years of doing this work, I have never felt stuck with the label of "minister" or "spiritual leader," as I know myself to be my Self: an intelligent, loving, creative, individualized expression of Infinite Intelligence, Love, and Creativity. Like Brother Lawrence, I am quite sure I could practice the Presence of God by washing the pots and pans, and I sometimes do.

What delights you? What would do if all the resources you needed were available for that pursuit? Do you realize you can bring meaning to any task and you may perceive a deeper purpose in whatever activity you have decided to engage? Perhaps one way to enter into this delight for life is to watch and learn from one of those little children who simply enter with an attitude of joy and without any sense of limits.

Even in harsh situations, we can and must find meaning if we are to remain connected to ourselves and others. An amazing example is the brilliant and brave psychiatrist, Viktor Frankl, who survived countless atrocities in a concentration camp and developed his practice of *logotherapy*, which helps others find meaning in life. Through logotherapy, young people who felt deprived in their early upbringing have been able to see the benefits of learning to develop their true capabilities and have proved to be role models for other disadvantaged children.

I have had the privilege of knowing people who have experienced physical disabilities yet whose indomitable spirits continue to bring meaning to their lives and the lives of others. In my regular visits to convalescent hospitals, I became friends with a 45-year-old man with a debilitating physical disease. Frank was confined to a wheelchair in which he had to be well secured. Speech was difficult, but he never gave up, making certain the person listening understood every word. Most remarkable was his ability to operate the ham radio in his room, which enabled him to make friends worldwide. Frank's patience with strangers he met on the airwaves amazed me, as he would eventually dispel their initial belief that they were speaking to a drunk. He taught me so much about being authentic (not pretending to understand if I did not) and increasing patience. I also delighted in his unusual laugh, which brought great joy to everyone in the room. His life had great meaning and purpose.

How are you expressing your great spirit in the world? You may wish to ask yourself a few questions about purpose and meaning. Listen deeply to yourself until you are inspired to expand your delight in living. Why not ask yourself:

1. *How much joy do I bring to my day?*

2. *What did I love to do as a child?*

3. *Is there an element of that passion I can incorporate in my life today?*

4. *What would cause me to spring out of bed in the morning?*

5. *How would I like to feel at the end of each day?*

6. *How may I live a more purposeful life?*

Why not say to yourself:

1. *I choose to connect with the joy within me and allow it to emerge.*

2. *I am ready to bring childlike delight to all I do.*

3. *I am free to live from the deepest passion of my heart.*

4. I enter into life consciously, confidently, and enthusiastically.

5. I invite myself to feel peaceful and grateful at day's end, knowing I've done my best.

6. I now decide to live my life on purpose, allowing myself to be guided to that which is for my greatest fulfillment.

Chapter

Twelve

Taking It Lightly

*E*verything is sacred; nothing is serious. I have used this phrase as my mantra since I first heard it many years ago, and I believe it to be true. I will admit having appropriated it from a colleague, and I trust she continues to live by it as well.

Perhaps you have heard the saying, "Angels can fly because they take themselves lightly." I find myself uplifted and inspired by teachers who smile much and criticize little, who walk in an atmosphere of happiness and ease, and who disseminate the Light of Truth with a sense of joy. The great spiritual teacher, Ernest Holmes, stated, "Take what you are doing seriously, but don't take yourself too seriously while you are doing it."

Just think of the enormous travails experienced by the Dalai Lama and his people, and still this wise and gentle soul approaches each day with sweet serenity, an irrepressible smile on his face, and a readiness to be the embodiment of joy. He is the perfect manifestation of the truth that, "Everything is sacred; nothing is serious," for he deeply honors all life. Great teachers tend to touch this place of Divine Joy and do their best to bring it forth from others.

An unusually effective teacher who helped me lighten up was another Berkeley character, often referred to as "The Bubble Lady." She walked the UC Berkeley campus, as well as the streets around Telegraph Avenue, dressed in long, velvety clothing, usually wearing a hat and carrying a pouch over her arm. Her jewelry was unique, and she looked a bit like a good witch. She was called "The Bubble Lady" because she was usually seen blowing bubbles with a wand from the same plastic bottles of soapy liquid children enjoy. The bubbles were often responsible for over-responsible students with large amounts of data in their heads suddenly finding their faces relaxing into smiles and their muscles letting go of term-paper tension.

I approached her one day to express my great appreciation for the lightness and joy she brought to our campus. Respectfully, I asked if my gratitude could take the form of making a contribution to her "bubble fund." Her response was, "Well, you could buy my book!" In her pouch, she carried a number of copies of her marvelous "street poetry," and I became a great fan, purchasing every new collection she created!

The Bubble Lady had a name: Julia Vinograd. She was a UC Berkeley alumna who had completed her graduate work at a prestigious midwestern university and returned to lift people's spirits on a daily basis. Thank you, Julia.

Too often, we take ourselves too seriously and take our mistakes too much to heart. Furrowed brows and premature wrinkles tend to emerge when we stay in regret or shame over what we may perceive as mistakes made in the past. Imagine, for a moment, the posture most people take when they are embarrassed by something they wish they had not done: the shoulders rounded, the head down, and a most unhappy look on the face. Now, recall what circus clowns do when they drop their props (usually on purpose) or step on each other's elongated shoes (always on purpose.) They stand tall, place their arms straight up in the air, and turn confidently from one portion of their audience to the next, usually with a loud, "Ta-da!"

Can you even imagine doing the latter the next time you begin to feel bad about a perceived failure or lapse of judgment? It is very healing and opens the way for a new and better scenario to be experienced the next time a similar event occurs. I believe it was Will Rogers who suggested we laugh at ourselves at least once a day, before 10:00 o'clock in the morning, and I never have any trouble with that one! My very wise teacher, Earl Barnum, used to tell me it takes about 101 muscles to frown and only about four to smile. He also told me that if a smile is suppressed and not permitted to form on the mouth, it will just slip down further and further on the body until it turns into big hips. This hilarity from one of the wisest, most loving and inspirational teachers I have ever known taught me to live lightly in order to live deeply and youthfully. I prefer laugh lines to worry wrinkles.

A liberating question we may ask ourselves when worried, anxious, or self-critical is: "What difference will this really make in ten years' time?" In most cases, the situation will not even be remembered a year from now, so why not lighten up, release it, and move confidently into a new attitude? Ralph Waldo Emerson suggested we ". . . take our bloated nothingness out of the path of the divine circuits." Let's begin trusting the Wise and Joyful Presence within to lift us above any unpleasant circumstance and keep us in innocent delight.

Why not ask yourself:

1. *Do I tend to take myself too seriously?*

2. *Do I smile and laugh often?*

3. *Do I forgive my foibles quickly?*

4. *Do I use humor to lift myself from negative situations?*

Why not say to yourself:

1. *Everything is sacred; nothing is serious.*

2. *I give myself permission to smile widely and laugh out loud.*

3. *I use gentle humor to forgive my mistakes completely and rise to joy.*

Chapter

Thirteen

What Works for You

*I*n sharing with you how I maintain my sense of
aliveness and the health of my mind and body, I
am quite aware and respectful of differences in life
situations and support the path of joy and wholeness
that is workable for you. Above all, I would ask that
you enter more fully into the flow of life, releasing
limiting and negative thoughts and becoming open
to a stream of fresh, inspiring, life-affirming ideas. By
connecting deeply with your Source and keeping your
mind and your body as flexible as possible, you are
allowing that stream of energy to supply you with a
sense of wellbeing and delight.

You need not spend hours working out in a gym if your
body responds well to gentler activities like walking
and swimming. Chair exercises are available for people
not yet accustomed to strenuous activities, and it is
better to find some form of movement than to remain
stuck in blocking life's natural flow. A triathlon may
not be on your schedule today, but you can certainly
find pleasurable movement and feel more alive and
vital.

If you do not have time just now to take a class or master a musical instrument, how about working daily crossword puzzles, guessing the proper responses to "Jeopardy," or challenging your friends to a game of cards to keep your mind alert and active? Our brains are hungry for challenging stimuli, and we do them a disservice by feeding them the junk so often served up on television. Opportunities abound to learn something new about another person, and the only tuition that needs to be paid is your close attention.

Rather than making a radical change in your food choices, you might consider becoming more conscious of what you are putting in your mouth during the day, eat only when you are hungry, and stop when you begin to feel full. If you really listen to your body, it will be glad to guide you to the foods that will nourish it properly and allow it to feel more light and comfortable. Agree to agree with your food, and fill up with more gratitude than calories.

If you are not yet drawn to sitting for 30 minutes in meditation, consider spending more time in nature by observing a flower, looking at the stars, or listening to the birdsongs. Begin to feel your connection with all living things, allowing yourself to experience the underlying unity of life. Extend an invitation to the wonders around you to stimulate your soul. Even a few moments of conscious, openhearted observation can reduce stress and bring you gently back to your natural sense of oneness with all.

I know a wonderful group of people who were trained by Sri Eknath Easwaren in a simple technique called "Passage Meditation," in which a sacred, inspirational reading is memorized and repeated slowly and silently. This practice stills the mind, giving it something uplifting on which to focus, while the heart opens to a greater connection. I met a woman who simply sings a meaningful chant while she prepares breakfast in the morning, just as I often repeat a silent mantra while walking.

Discovering and releasing just one resentment or regret each day will begin to free up space in your heart for conscious choices, healthy thoughts and feelings, rewarding activities, and delightful relationships. Replacing one limiting belief with an affirmative statement is a powerful beginning to a transformative life filled with greater possibilities. Surely within each 24-hour period you will be able and willing to release one or more stumbling blocks to your greater fulfillment and invite them to become steppingstones to your more youthful expression of life.

You may not yet feel able to love unconditionally, forgive instantly, or connect on a deep level with every person you meet, but you can begin to look for something of value within everyone you know. Finding something to appreciate within one or more people is an easy daily practice that can lead to wonderfully satisfying relationships. If you have not yet come to acknowledge your own specialness, today would be a good day to notice how valuable and lovable you are as well.

Now, if you do feel ready to move dynamically into a greater version of yourself, if you are taking those dreams off the shelf, and if you already feel the stirring of expansive life within your heart and soul, then choose to move confidently into your magnificence. As Goethe shared, "Whatever you can do or dream, begin it. Boldness has genius, power, and magic in it."

Chapter Fourteen

Encouraging Examples

The following true stories of encouragement were sent to me over the past three years and are reprinted here with permission. Most were sent by attendees of my "Alive and Ageless" workshop, which I conducted at a spiritual retreat at the Asilomar conference center on the Monterey Peninsula in California.

I honor every account of living an unlimited life at any age. The examples include celebrating physical health and fortitude, serendipitously meeting a soulmate, adventuring into new territory, and simply delighting in the joy of expanded living. These wonderful individuals know what it means to be "youthing"—as opposed to aging—and they have tapped into a great wellspring of infinite aliveness. Let them inspire you as they have inspired me.

Lucretia Cooper

I was 67 in 2003 when my third husband died. It had been a tumultuous relationship, and I was almost to the point of accepting that I would leave this plane without ever finding true love. I had been told that after 60, there were so many more available women than men that there was not much chance for me. Even so, I continued to add to my list of desired qualities in a man—the kind of man I wanted to attract into my life.

Not knowing where to meet single men my age in the small town where I live, I turned to the Internet. I had fun browsing and looking at bios, and even going out from time to time, but no real match.

Then one day I got an email from a site telling me of a man who met my requested criteria. I took a look at his profile and tried to dismiss him—his picture looked so dorky! However, the Universe would not let that happen. I got "Truth chills." That was my signal to act, so I sent the guy an email, and he responded in less that an hour! We set up a time and place to have coffee. We met at 2:00 p.m. the next day, talking until the coffee shop closed at 6:00. Then we went to dinner and closed the restaurant, too.

In our first conversation, I told him my spiritual life was very important, and he offered to go to church with me the following Sunday. Halfway through the service, I glanced over at him, and tears were rolling down his cheeks. My first thought was, "This one is a keeper!" He definitely is a keeper, and we have been together for five glorious years and are as in love as we were the first week. We are active and travel with our tandem bike, having cycled in Ireland, Scotland, and Spain, as well as Oregon, Washington, Illinois, Arizona, Vermont, and Kentucky. Herb is now my husband, and we are both 72. The cycling keeps us in fabulous shape, and I weigh about what I did when I graduated from high school. I am truly "youthing." Life is Good. Love keeps you young.

Roger Emanuels

Growing up in the country, not far from the urban San Francisco Bay Area, my childhood was filled with outdoor adventures and unlimited space to explore and enjoy. The family home was situated in a large, level valley planted in walnuts, where my grandparents joined other farmers to take advantage of the rich, fertile soil. The large valley was surrounded by oak-studded hills, and the North face of magnificent Mount Diablo loomed over all.

On my tenth birthday, a large strawberry roan mare was a gift from my parents. "Little Joe," as she was introduced to me, was beautiful and spirited. With questionable training, she was inappropriate for a ten-year-old, but she was wonderful. On our first day together, she ran away with me in the saddle and dumped me headfirst into a freshly plowed orchard. Over the next five years, many family members and friends had bad experiences with her, the worst being my broken arm at age 12 when she swerved in a run, leaving me again in the orchard.

Nevertheless, Little Joe became a trusted friend who followed me around without a rope, hoping for an apple or carrot treat. I talked to her as though she understood my childhood dreams and concerns. I learned a lot from my horse, especially confidence and balance. I was never a particularly brave youngster—I didn't even enjoy a ride on the roller coaster—but somehow, I never feared my horse as we got to know each other.

Eventually, my parents tired of the spills and accidents, and they traded Little Joe for a smaller, docile, unresponsive mare I couldn't communicate with. I began to lose interest in horses. Soon, I obtained a drivers license. I found a part time job after school and bought my brother's Ford when he left for college. That was 1957. My childhood was over. Now I could look ahead to becoming an adult. Horses were for children.

Nearly 50 years later, I traveled to southern Chile. A three-day excursion by horse to a mountain lodge sounded inviting, but how could I survive a five-hour ride up a muddy trail to the lodge? I decided to give it a try, out of curiosity more than anything else. To my surprise, I survived the ride easily, having no trouble keeping my balance when the horse skidded on the trail or jumped over a log. Riding was just as fun as it was when I was a boy!

Over the past several years, I have been able to enjoy great horse trips in South America and even Mongolia. Every day on horseback is a day without a car or other mechanical transportation. Like riding a bicycle, it seems quite natural to be on the back of a horse. To maneuver in difficult terrain, I prefer the four strong legs of a horse to my two aging legs. I seem to bond with each horse that carries me up and down muddy trails, much as I did with my beloved Little Joe all those years ago.

Jane Claypool

Not only did I have a difficult childhood, I was widowed twice by the young age of 33. I recall sitting in a park at 35, saying to my sister, "I feel at least 100 years old." At that point of emotional exhaustion, I began my spiritual journey, doing inner, personal exploration, as well as studying psychology. Noticing I was feeling younger and younger, I realized that at age 45, I actually felt much younger than I had ten years earlier!

Aging did not bother me until I experienced the limitation of an illness; yet, even now, I am better equipped to handle it than I would have been at 35, and I'm feeling happier, more hopeful, and, in many ways, younger than ever.

Joseph Lynn Anderson

I began running in my early forties as a way to lose weight and kick a heavy tobacco addiction. I accomplished both goals. I completed numerous five-, ten-, and 15-mile runs. Over those years, I developed a goal to run a marathon (26.2 miles) but I did not realize that special goal until I was 63 years old. The closer I got to retirement, the more I began to believe I would never run my marathon.

I shared my frustration with a friend who was a marathoner. He assured me anyone my age (assuming I had no physical limitations) could run a marathon, and he volunteered to develop a training program to prepare me. I followed a four-month training program that included daily runs, most days beginning at 5:30 a.m. Initially, I ran only 30 to 60 minutes per day, but by the end of the program, I was running four-and-a-half hours and covering more than 20 miles.

I completed my training program and registered to run the Portland Oregon Marathon in September 2000. Crossing the finish line and seeing my family and friends cheering me on was very special to me. It also happened that I was celebrating my 63rd birthday. For many people, setting and achieving goals is why they wake up each morning and get on with their lives.

Three years ago, I developed Parkinson's, a progressive and chronic disease that has no cure. At the same time, studies show that exercise can slow down the progression. I turn 72 this year, and my primary goal is to walk an hour each day and continue to enjoy the journey.

Jozella Fargher

My experience with age has been measured in tens. Approaching the beginning of my eighth decade, I look back in amazement at each of those ten-year spans and realize how exciting and life-changing they all were. Rather than viewing the approaching era with apprehension, I feel confident and empowered. I take the next journey with complete faith, based on my previous experiences, and I know God won't drop me now! A brief review of my life might be sung to Old Blue Eyes' "September Song," but mine is more fun!

When I was 20, I was a new and unwed mother, and life had taken a twist for what seemed to be "the worst." This major life change I now see as a blessing that improved and possibly saved my life, as I was forced into a maturity I could not have found had I continued in my destructive ways. At 30, I suffered the "I'll always be 29" syndrome, but 30 was "the new 20," and it was the year of my Cinderella marriage to the love of my life and the beginning of a worldwide adventure.

Then 40 arrived, and I no longer saw myself as a "cute little thing," but felt over the hill, as I was divorced from that same Cinderella story man and had to start my life over completely, traveling 3,500 miles from those adventures back to my home state with very little money and no job, trying to furnish an apartment with cheap garage-sale furniture. On turning 50, I began to think of my life as "half over," yet I was living a sober, mature life with more ups than downs, and I was not looking for excitement. Another Mr. Wonderful wanted to marry me, and I decided to have a run at it—and run I did! This marriage introduced me to the rugged outdoors. I became a 10K race runner and avid backpacking hiker, and was in better shape than I had been in my entire life!

As this marriage went sour, I came to realize that I'd had a great life, was happy with the woman I'd become, and was grateful for all my journeys.

At 60, I met "the one"—the one God had hidden under a different rock, the one I would never have picked, and the one who has provided me with the best life ever. It's so good that there are moments when I wonder, "How could this be?" because it's like a dream. Today, I am nearly seventy, and I'm still here! Bring it on!

Tina Wilding

When I was 52, my husband gave me scuba diving lessons for Christmas. He is something of a "fish," loving to swim, wind surf, and sail. I, on the other hand, am more of a scaredy cat!

The local dive shop has a classroom where my classmates and I learned the "theory" portion of the class. In the next room, which can be seen through the classroom window, there is a dive tank. This is where students put on gear and enter the water for the remaining five lessons.

My first day in the water did not go well, as I could not wrap my mind around the idea of trusting the regulator to breathe. I phoned the instructor that night to ask if anyone had ever dropped out after the first class. She kindly informed me that she would be very patient with me and would not make me do anything until I was ready.

Knowing how important it was to my husband to be able to share these experiences with me, I decided to use affirmative prayer, remembering the Loving Intelligence of the Universe is present everywhere—on land and in the water! I also affirmed that I had the courage, strength, and intelligence to learn and do anything I desired.

I completed all five classes, receiving a grade of 100% on the theory and succeeding with all the skills. I even went to the Caribbean and completed four open-water dives to receive my certification. In that water, 65 feet down, I truly felt ageless and alive. My husband said I was leading the way and all the other divers were following me! I stretched my comfort zone and experienced a bliss I never would have experienced otherwise. I am excited about our next trip to Belize when I'll be a mere 55!

Denise Kaku

Part of change has been examining my limiting beliefs and doing something new that invigorates and excites me. So, at the age of 58, I joined an Aikido dojo after first getting a bone scan and assessing my level of health fitness. After three years of practice, I can, indeed, continue this peaceful martial art for as long as my spirit is willing. I chose this particular physical practice because of my training as a somatic leadership coach. I have found the rigorous commitment and consistency of practicing Aikido is a wonderful way to be aware of how I move from my centered presence, which supports my promise to live more boldly!

Virginia Mudd

The idea to climb the Grand Tetons to commemorate my sixtieth year began when I was 35. I had gone to the Jackson Lake Lodge for a haircut at the end of a 42-day solo bike trip from my home in the San Francisco Bay Area to Jackson Hole, Wyoming.

A woman in the salon told me she had climbed the Grand Teton—the tallest and most majestic of the range—when she was 60. This struck me as an incredible thing to do once a person tottered into Old Age! While the scissors snipped my hair, I decided I would do the same thing. At the time, I probably didn't think I'd ever be "old."

When 2008 rolled around, it was a sure thing I would turn 60, so in keeping with my 25-year intention and promise, I signed up with a guide service nine months prior to my desired climb date. Exum Mountain Guides required two days of mountaineering training before qualifying a person to climb the Grand Teton. With their help, I made a plan: training classes August 2 and 3, rest day August 4, then climb the Grand August 5 and 6, 2009.

I started my own getting-in-shape program in April. First, I had to rehab a "frozen shoulder," undergoing six weeks of physical therapy to stretch-out and strengthen my right shoulder. Then on to running, vigorous horse riding, pumping iron, working out in my home gym, and, finally, rock climbing school at the local gym. Mental training was about staying positive, not scaring myself by looking at pictures of vertical walls I'd have to climb, and trying to believe I could do it. By August 1, I was feeling very fit and as ready as I could be. I would soon learn it was a fraction of the fitness and endurance I would need for the climb.

Exum Mountaineering Level I and II was not summer camp. The guides made it clear that the climbing students would not be mollycoddled. We were expected to tie knots, rappel down cliffs, safely belay our partner, climb vertical rock faces of 30 to 40 feet, and clearly communicate on the windy summit of the Grand. We had to move efficiently and safely over rocky terrain, stay calm and present, and handle ourselves in stressful circumstances. At the conclusion of school, I was already sore, overloaded with information, and nervous, but relieved and thrilled that I qualified for the Grand climb!

I made it to the summit at 13,770 feet. It took seven hours to hike the seven and a half miles to base camp, 5,000 feet in elevation gain, where we spent the night. The following morning at 4:30, we climbed another 2,150 feet up to the summit in four hours, then all the way back "home" the same day in another six hours.

It was the hardest thing I've ever done—a huge stretch mentally and physically. It took three weeks for my thigh muscles to stop hurting, and the inner journey is far from over. I am amazed that I did it. It was an exhilarating, terrifying, and amazing experience. I wonder what unusual venture I will think up 25 years from now when I'm really old.

Joy Ryan

On June 28, 1992, when I was 49, I arrived in Vancouver and met 45 other cyclists to begin a 7,500 kilometer trek across Canada. As a fairly inexperienced cyclist, I was excited but somewhat apprehensive to begin my first long tour. The ages of the cyclists ranged from 17 to 65, a rather mature group that included eight people in their 40s, 11 in their 50s, and six in their 60s. Equal numbers of men and women represented nearly every Canadian province, with one person from England and another from the U.S.

The first day began rather slowly, and after pitching our tents that night, a torrential rain began that lasted 12 days and nights! Much of the beauty of Hope, Merritt, Kamloops, and Revelstoke was lost in fog, and I experienced extreme cold as rain turned into hail the size of chicken eggs. Suffering from hypothermia, I arrived at a camp without hot water. The other cyclists used the restroom hand dryer to thaw me out, repeatedly pushing the "on" button for the warm air to circulate.

Traveling through Saskatchewan, we cycled with a fierce wind on our backs, which was actually helpful. Then, the rain came down again, and we arrived at a flooded-out campsite.

The weather improved as we left Manitoba and ventured into Ontario. I began feeling miserable and weak with the flu, losing control of my bike on the rough shoulder and ending up in the ditch. X-rays showed that, in addition to the flu, I now had two cracked ribs along with the scrapes and bruises. I don't remember much of New Brunswick because of the pain. The tour was now almost over, and I chose to persevere and finish, never, ever thinking of quitting.

The last day, in St. John's, Newfoundland, in freezing temperatures, our last obstacle to overcome was a long climb up a winding, steep hill. Most of us had to walk our bikes to the top. One by one, we all finally made it up. We threw our arms around each other, jubilantly congratulating one another and exclaiming: "We have crossed over the finish line!"

What an accomplishment! To celebrate my 65th birthday, I plan to hike in Liechtenstein, and the following year will find me on a 100-mile hike in the Highlands in Scotland. I am "youthing!"

Chapter
Fifteen

Drawing a Conclusion

$\mathcal{M}$y purpose in sharing these words with you—my own and those of others—is to assist in awakening you to greater spiritual aliveness and physical vitality. Nothing gives me greater joy than to facilitate and witness the release of false or limiting beliefs and support your willingness to live fully, joyously, and productively at any and every age.

Once we learn how to tap into the Source of Boundless Energy and Wisdom, it becomes easier to discover new ways and means of living from our passion and bliss. Not only do our lives become more fulfilled, we become radiant examples for others, showing them possibilities beyond their present understanding. Looking good, feeling well, enjoying healthy relationships, releasing limiting beliefs, and setting an intention to move forward with joy all engender a bright outlook and a satisfying life experience here and now.

We needn't remain constricted by false beliefs, either those of the world or those of our own making, because there is a greater truth to be known and lived. You are valuable, intelligent, and capable beyond your present awareness, and you have a great deal to give and receive for the rest of your life, whether you count it in days or decades.

Find what makes your heart sing, and invite the Infinite Source of Life to fill you with inspiration and creativity.

With all my heart, I encourage you to live deeply and largely, letting your Inner Spirit guide you to real freedom and aliveness. In making a commitment to embrace a life of new possibility, you may wish to begin with a two-week period in which you consider naming each day and becoming more aware of the ideas we have discussed here:

Day #1: "Boundless Energy" — Find something about which you truly can feel enthusiastic, and bring keen interest to everything you do.

Day #2: "Forever Young" — See your world through the eyes of a child today, bringing real delight to each moment.

Day #3: "Living in the Flow" — Experience yourself as a recirculating fountain of life, mentally, physically, and emotionally.

Day #4: "Looking Good" — Practice smiling throughout the day, silently and sweetly experiencing the peace and joy of it.

Day #5: "Conscious Eating" — Be more mindful of your attitude and actions regarding food, gently noticing and wisely making good choices.

Day #6: "The Joy of Movement" — Feel yourself move more gracefully, aligning with universal balance and harmony as you appreciate and enjoy your body.

Day #7: "Impossible Dreams" — Allow yourself 15 minutes today to review unfilled aspirations that still lift your heart, then choose to bring one down from the shelf of your mind and focus on it.

Day #8: "Transforming Outworn Beliefs" — Choose one limiting belief you realize no longer serves you; consciously and lovingly discard it, then replace it with a constructive one.

Day #9: "Creative Connections" — Practice experiencing yourself as an essential part of all life, seeing yourself in others and others in you. Feel your infinite connection with all life, and praise all sentient beings.

Day #10: "Love, Value, and Creativity" — Allow yourself to love and be loved; feel your worth, allow others to express your value to you; and, find meaningful ways to be creative today.

Day #11: *"Meaning and Purpose"* — View the world through the eyes of possibility today, allowing yourself to be amazed and delighted with everything and everyone around you.

Day #12: *"Keeping It Light"* – Breathe more deeply, smile more widely, and forgive yourself and others more quickly today. Remember the "Ta-da!" approach to supposed mistakes.

Day #13: *"What Works for You"* — Choose one thing today that you can happily and honestly add to or delete from your life, and live from a place of ease and gratitude.

Day #14: *"Encouraging Examples"* — Look around you and note the accomplishments of friends, neighbors, and people in the media that may inspire you to look beyond your present situation to new possibilities. Then, become an encouraging example to others.

Let's continue this adventure together! I always welcome your personal stories of living fully in the awareness of being Alive and Ageless!

For more information and to keep in touch, contact me via my website at:

www.TheConsciousConnections.com

About the
Author

Dr. Maxine Kaye

Dr. Maxine Kaye is a popular presenter known for her dynamic classes and seminars. For 35 years, she has been revered as a teacher, spiritual director, couples counselor, speaker, and author. She is sought-after as a facilitator for workshops and retreats and is an officiant for weddings, christenings, and life celebrations (memorials).

Alive and Ageless: How to Feel Alive and Live Fully Every Day of Your Life is her first book. Her writing has inspired a number of workshops, which she presents all across the United States and Canada.

Whether assisting people in connecting more deeply to their Source, to their passion, or to one another, Dr. Maxine is a gentle and effective spiritual director and facilitator, both in one-on-one sessions and in classrooms or retreat centers.

Classes in expansive and effective living are listed on her website, as well as speaking and workshop dates and locations nationwide.

Dr. Maxine offers a daily inspirational message Monday through Friday. Contact her at dr.maxine@ theconsciousconnections.com, by telephone at (760) 574-2490, or by visiting her website:

www.TheConsciousConnections.com